50 FREE smiles

50 FREE smiles

VERY, VERY CHEAP HINTS FOR HAPPINESS

Susannah Mac

The Five Mile Press

The Five Mile Press Pty Ltd
1 Centre Road, Scoresby
Victoria 3179 Australia
www.fivemile.com.au

Copyright © Susannah Mac, 2009
All rights reserved

First published 2009

Printed in China

Designed by Kristy Lund

ISBN 978 1 74211 975 5

National Library of Australia Cataloguing in Publication Data:

    Mac, Susannah.
    50 free smiles : very, very cheap hints for happiness /

    Susannah Mac.

    978 1 74211 975 5 (pbk)

    Happiness.
    Life skills.
    Social skills.
    Conduct of life.

    158.1

For Jane Tewson
Expert smile-maker, who started it all

50% of all author royalties will go to Pilotlight Australia
www.pilotlight.org.au

Smiling is infectious,

You can catch it like the flu.

Someone smiled at me today,

And I started smiling too.

Author unknown

Smile

Just smile.

Think a happy thought and turn your mouth upwards.

It takes fewer muscles to smile than it does to frown, and it makes you 'think happy'.

If you smile at someone, it's more than likely they'll smile back (don't do it too intensely, though — in some big cities, it may seem a bit stalker-like).

And it's free. Actually, when did the best things in life stop being free?

Maybe they didn't; maybe we just got distracted.

Real happiness rarely comes in a box. Lots of things that make us smile don't cost a cent. And lots of things that make us smile make other people smile – in fact, research into happiness (it's a serious science this happiness) shows that people who help others are happier. People who give get — if you get what I mean.

So maybe we should take a minute to think about what makes us smile, really smile. Happiness doesn't just happen — we can find it, build it, keep it.

Here are some ideas, some little thought starters to get you going. Try them. Share them. Find more and share them, too.

Here's to happiness — yours, mine, everyone's.

Smile!

Tell a good joke

Laughing is good for us and, funnily enough, fun.

Learn and remember 10 really good jokes — five of which could be told to a 10-year-old, or your mother.

Here's one to get you started:
Q. What's brown and sticky?
A. A stick.

Count your blessings

Be thankful.

In the Buddhist teachings:

'For if we didn't learn a lot, at least we learned a little, and if we didn't learn a little, at least we didn't get sick, and if we did get sick, at least we didn't die, so let us all be thankful.'

So every day find five things to be thankful for:

A healthy child.
A lovely sunset.
A winning football team.
A nice cup of tea.
A song that makes us want to dance.

You get the idea?

Try it.

Walk
run
skip jog
hop

Get your heart rate up and your endorphins out.

When we exercise we feel better — maybe not always during, but certainly after.

A little every day is a start. A bit more every day is even better.

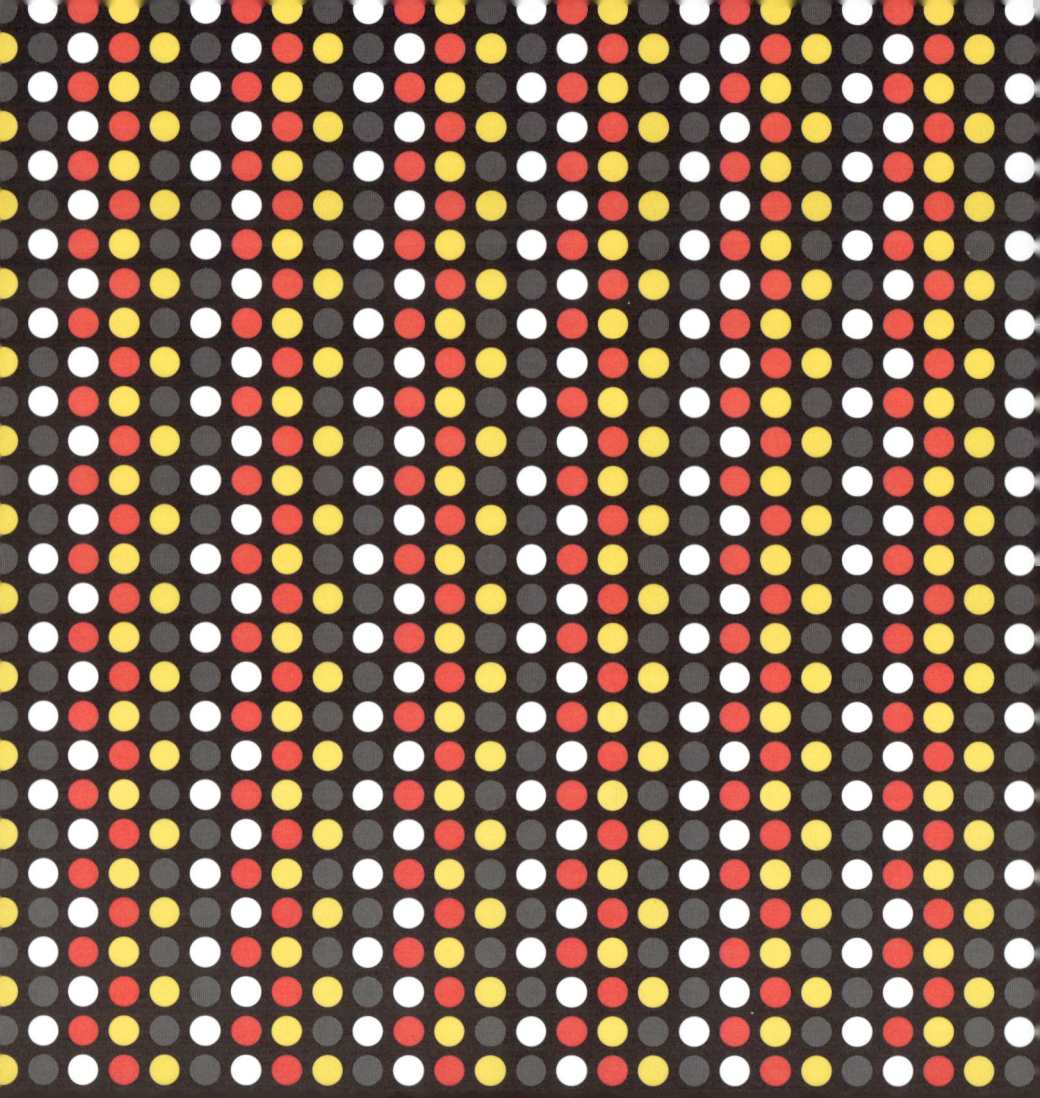

'We make a living by
what we get,
but we make a life
by what we give'

Winston Churchill

Sometimes the best way to make
ourselves happy is to make others happy.

Give blood

You can save a life.

Other people desperately need your blood. It takes only a little time and you will soon make more of it. And they give you biscuits!

Make it a social event — organise some friends, a group from work.

Go online or ring your local blood bank.

Give your spare time

Give your time and get more than you bargained for back. Helping people is healthy and makes you feel fabulous. It makes other people feel pretty good, too.

There are so many ways you can volunteer. Read for the blind. Help out at your local school, your local nursing home, your local crisis centre. Use your skills, muscles and time to help a not-for-profit company. Make it a family thing.

Get online and search volunteering to get started.

Go ahead, make someone's day — and yours.

Make lists of things you love

What are your top 10 songs?

Top 10 books?
Top 10 films?
Top 10 foods?
Top 10 advertising jingles?
Top 10 best inventions?
Top 10 sports people ever?

Share or argue for your favourites with family and friends.

Get things out in the open

Open the blinds.

Open the window.

Open the door.

Open your eyes.

Open your heart.

Open your mind.

Opening one is a great start, but imagine what might happen if you opened them all?

Lose or find yourself in a book

Read a book.

Re-read a childhood favourite, or maybe work your way through the classics. Read your mum's favourite book. Your best friend's.

Swap books with friends.

Join a library. Pick a cover that takes your fancy or ask the librarian for help.

Disappear into another world for a few hours.

Join or start a club

A food club.

A book club.

A chess club.

A music club.

A wine club.

A knitting club.

They are all just good excuses to catch up, to connect.

Share your interests with your friends. Make new friends. Make new interests.

Close your eyes. Breathe deeply

Take just three minutes of your time, even one.

Close your eyes and take deep breaths. Think only about your breathing and let other thoughts go out with your breath.

Take time to be still, re-balance.

You might like it — find out more about meditation, yoga, Pilates.

Or just keep your eyes closed a bit longer and take another breath.

Get wet

Go for a swim — in the ocean, a river, even a swimming pool.

Float for a while or do a few laps. Either way, enjoy the sense of the water around you — and no mobile phone can reach you underwater.

If you can't swim, maybe now's the time to learn.

Commune with nature

Take a walk in a garden, a park, a forest, by the beach.

Don't worry about the destination — enjoy the ride and take in the beautiful things around you. The smells, the sounds, the sights.

A flower blooming or a tree blossoming.

Ducks quacking on a lake.

Cloud shapes in the sky.

A butterfly.

Discover your own backyard

Well, you can go a little further. When was the last time you walked down your street, around your block?

We often take those things closest to home for granted but now 'staycations' are the new vacations! Discover what your suburb, your city has to offer.

What is important to you?

Don't wait for tragedy to strike to remind you — remind yourself!

Remember no-one ever lay on their death bed wishing that they'd stayed longer at the office or ironed more shirts.

Write down what's important to you. Do you spend enough time looking after it?

Spring clean

Your wallet.

Your bag.

Your desk.

Your room.

Your flat.

Your mind.

Talk less, listen more

Listen to your kids, your parents, your partner, your friends.

Really listen, rather than just wait to talk again.

Ask more questions — and wait for the answer. (How many times do we pass someone and ask 'How are you going?' without stopping to find out?)

Ask your parents about their childhood, about your childhood. What did your dad want to do when he grew up?
Do you know?

Learn something new

It doesn't have to be Spanish or neurosurgery — but it might be.

It might also be how to use chopsticks, how to change a tyre, give a really good massage, whistle the national anthem, make an origami anything.

Learn a new word every day.

Do it with other people.

Try it.

Let music rev you up

Or calm you down.

Sing it, hum it, listen to it, play it, dance to it.

Do it all at once.

Discover a new music style. Crump to a classic. Waltz to Wolfmother.

What songs would be on the soundtrack of your life?

Plant something — watch it grow

Grow a vegetable garden or just a vegetable on your window sill.

You can feed a family from a square metre of vegie patch.

Or brighten your day with just one flower.

Plant a seed and watch it take shape, unfold.

Plant a native tree and offset your greenhouse emissions — ask your local council how.

Join a team sport

Football, netball, touch rugby, table tennis, baseball, rounders, hockey, softball, lacrosse, cricket, bowls, badminton …

Take up a childhood sport again, try a new one.

There are clubs all over town.

Do it with a group of friends or make new ones when you join.

Try it. Try out.

Bring back 'bring a plate'

Invite friends to dinner and invite them to bring some of it!

Make it a regular thing. There's nothing like eating and laughing with friends — and everyone shares the load.

Have an afternoon tea where everyone brings a plate — and the recipe.

Feed your mind

Many museums and galleries are free and just waiting for you to discover them.

You might even be able to pop into one in your lunch hour.

Take some time just to wander the rooms, join a free tour.

Sit in front of a painting that takes your fancy and let your thoughts drift away.

Write a letter

Not an email, a letter.

Enjoy the paper, ink on the page, the envelope, the stamp.

Share a thought with someone you like, someone you love, someone you admire.

Remember **happy times**

Look at old photos and let the memories come back.

Happy times, laughter, holidays, conversations, special people.

The world always looks brighter behind a smile.

Op swap

Take your old clothes to the local op shop and see if you might pick up something yourself there — someone's rejects are someone else's vintage.

Re-discover your old things — bring them back into your life or put them into someone else's.

Make something

Bread, jam, paper, aeroplane.

Display it, give it away, fly it.

(But just don't make a mountain out of a molehill about it.)

Get stuck in a routine

No equipment, no gym, no personal trainer, no lycra (unless you really want to) but perhaps a little motivation.

Set the alarm just a little bit earlier and make up your own routine. Don't do any exercise you don't like, or your doctor wouldn't want you to.

In less than half an hour, you will have got both your body and brain working up a gear and ready to start the day.

Try a —

10-minute jog.

10 minutes of exercises (maybe push-ups, lunges, sit-ups).

5-minute jog with the last minute fast.

1 minute intense self-congratulation.

Do it with your kids, your partner, your flatmates, your dog.

Or just enjoy the quiet time by yourself.

It opens up your lungs and fills your heart.

Sing with someone else. Sing in rounds — start with 'Row, Row, Row Your Boat' and work your way up to 'Bohemian Rhapsody'.

Join a choir.

Or just belt out a song in the shower.

Forgive someone

Sometimes it's the things that we don't do that can stop us being happy.

We can be angry, we can resent, we can stew and bear a grudge.

Or maybe, sometimes, we can let it go and forgive.

Have sex

Safely, with someone you want to (and who wants to have sex with you).

Get out of your comfort zone

Do one thing a day that challenges you.

Confront a fear, do something differently, try something new.

Walk around the park the wrong way.

Take the stairs not the lift.

Try something new for lunch.

Phone someone rather than email.

33

Draw, paint, scribble, scribe, sketch, sculpt, colour in.

Everyone is creative, some people just don't realise it.

It's a great way to unwind.

Find your creative self.

Giggle, chuckle, titter, guffaw, cackle, hoot, whoop.

At a joke.

At a funny show on TV.

At yourself.

Lighten up and laugh — it feels good.

And if all else fails, get someone to tickle you.

Make biscuits

Double the quantity to eat and share.

Take some into work, next door or to the local school.

Here's a simple recipe to get you going —

125 g butter
1 cup self-raising flour
½ cup sugar
½ cup custard powder
1 cup coconut
1 egg

Pre-heat oven to 180 degrees.

Mix everything together and roll into little balls.

Flatten balls onto tray lined with baking paper.

Bake 10–15 minutes or until golden and smelling yummy.

If you want, you can top with jam or choc bits before you put in oven. Or maybe something else — experiment!

Eat, share.

Call a friend

Leave the extra work, the ironing, the odd job and take the time to catch up and keep a friend.

Don't worry if it's been a long time — they will understand. After all, they haven't rung either!

If you can't call, send a text.

Pat or cuddle an animal

preferably a baby animal

Animals, especially baby ones, remind us of how simple and innocent things can be.

They are soft and cuddly.

Human babies are quite good cuddle therapy, too — just ask the parents first.

Eat happy food

Some foods are high in a natural chemical called tryptophan which converts in the body to feel-good serotonin.

Bananas, sunflower seeds, pineapple, tofu, spinach, peas and beans, eggs, chicken, sardines are happy foods.

It's probably not surprising they are all also natural foods, with no additives and little cooking.

So get fresh.

39

Slee

We need sleep. Most of us need more than we get.

Sleep lets us recharge. Re-boost. Re-energise. Our bodies and our brains.

Go to bed one hour earlier than you normally do.

Feel rested. Better.

Mow your neighbour's (or neighbours') lawn

Bring in their rubbish bins.

Remove their junk mail.

Drink water

Not out of a bottle — from a tap.

Drink two litres a day and keep your body hydrated and cleansed.

Feel better.

Never buy bottled water again (we survived for centuries without it).

Save water

Take showers not baths.

Take three-minute showers.

Turn the tap off while you brush your teeth.

Don't blush — share a flush (within hygienic reason, of course).

Don't rinse your plates, soak them.

Don't run dishwashers or washing machines half full.

Save the planet

Ok, well, not the whole planet and not completely by yourself.

But we know that every little bit helps and everything we do does make a difference.

Say thank you

It's not just a manners thing, it's a gratitude thing.

It's not an automatic response, it's letting someone know you appreciate them.

Someone who helped you.

Someone who cooked your meal.

Someone who let you in in the traffic.

Someone who rang to see how you were going.

Do a random act of kindness

Let someone who only has one item ahead of you in the supermarket queue.

Hold the door open for someone with a pram.

Stop to let someone cross the road.

Be on the lookout for opportunities.

Remember your inner child

Sometimes we take things too seriously and forget to do what kids do without thinking — play.

Play a practical joke (whoopee cushions are pretty foolproof) — who's going to ground you?

Play games.

Tell knock-knock jokes.

If you have them, show your kids your inner child, but maybe only at home — we wouldn't want to embarrass them… or would we?

47

Say sorry

Not 'sorry but I was angry'.

Not 'sorry but you were irritating me'.

Not 'sorry but I was rushing'.

No buts. Just sorry, a real sorry. Sorry I wish I hadn't done that and I want to make it up to you.

You won't be the only person to feel better.

Not so hard, with practice.

Hug
someone

Pretty much anyone, really. Put your arms around them and squeeze.

Have a hug checklist — Mum, Dad, kids, friends.

It's probably best to make it someone you know.

Become an organ donor

Only when you don't need them any more. Obviously.

But if you are, sadly, no longer using them, why not let them change or save someone else's life? What an amazing gift.

Think about registering. Discuss it with your family.

...

every day as if it is your last — because one day it will be.

There may be a lot you can't change, but there is also a lot you can.

Starting with your face muscles.

So smile!

The End

Or the beginning?

E...